Lotta Gessner

Late Night Musings

*Bibliografische Information der Deutschen Nationalbibliothek: Die
Deutsche Nationalbibliothek verzeichnet diese Publikation in der
Deutschen Nationalbibliografie; detaillierte bibliografische Daten sind im
Internet über <u>dnb.dnb.de</u> abrufbar.*

© 2022 Lotta Gessner
Herstellung und Verlag: BoD – Books on Demand, Norderstedt

ISBN: 9783756219940

Chapters

Roots

I'm not a brave person.

I am terrified, and picking at my lips 'til they bleed.

You're like an old tree – your roots are a tangled mess, wrapped around my heart, holding it in your twigs.

You are the dirt in my mouth. You're the moss in my hair and the sun caressing my skin.

You are hope and pain and a haven.

You are a rumbling river barely fast enough to pull me with you – but you did.

The wind is your heartbeat, resting in my lungs.

You could snap me if you'd wanted to but instead your roots are wrapped around me like armour, when the world is too big for me you keep me safe, and when the people are too loud you cover my ears and sing to me in the rumble of the ground.

I want to give that back to you.

I want to offer you my branches and my blooms, I want to be the moss in your hair and the sun on your skin and no matter where life takes me –

I want you in it.

In these woods we wander

The moss under our feet is soft as velvet,
and heavy leaves swallow the light.
Up this hill now, there is a temple,
dorian marble columns and a broken door,
a reminder of the people long since gone.
Come with me, love,
let us explore what they left behind.
Follow a creek, clear as crystal,
a fox with orange fur flees our footsteps,
an owl blinks lazily down at us.
Beyond the creek there is a mill
moving masses of water on its wooden wheel,
and down the path we find heavy rocks,
witnesses of centuries past.
Let us rest on their mossy surface,
watch the wind rustle the leaves
in these woods we wander quietly,
just the two of you and me.

Dear Baby Me

Dear Baby Me...

Boy, are you in for some trouble. Ooooh boy.

I wish I could tell you your life will be easy but – yeah no, that's not what's gonna happen.

You'll have plenty of happy times, don't you worry, but it will take years for you to find yourself. Like, I'm still not quite there.

It will take years and fears and tears, it will take people cutting you and stealing from you and throwing rocks at you and leaving you and abusing you until you finally find yourself – or part of it. But the important part is you will live to come out at the other end. You won't be stuck under the castle or with the dragons. You will defeat your demons and find magic in the trees and you will find friends that love you.

You are so strong, baby, you are so so strong.

I can't wait for you to meet

You

Dear

Remember me, dear
when our bodies turn to worm food
remember, dear
when nobody else does.
Have faith in me, dear
when my heart is way too heavy
just lean on me, dear
when it seems too painful to care.
Dance with me, dear
even when no music is playing
sing with me, dear
in defiance of those who muffle us.
Let me paint your picture, dear
even though anatomy fails me
let me draw you, dear
your eyes and hair and face a thousandfold.
Let me count them, dear
the freckles painting stars on your skin
let me see them, dear
all your imperfections and your flaws.

Take a rest with me, dear

let me take away your sorrows

rest your head in my lab, dear

fall asleep knowing you are safe.

Hear my plea, dear

my begging to be heard

see my colours, dear

and I pray you do not hate me for them.

Remember me, dear

when our bodies turn to ashes

remember me, dear,

when all that's left is dirt.

Mornings are my favourite Hour

Mornings are my favourite hour,

when we lay next to one another

and the sun is still asleep.

Your hair tickles my face

as your head rests on my shoulder;

we are safe here, darling,

and in these early hours when the world

seems far and the people miles away,

time does not yet exist.

The light is blue and purple,

there are no golden sunbeams yet,

there are no sounds but birds in the trees,

and I wish this moment could last an eternity.

I would guard our mornings like they were gold,

intricately spun.

Mornings are my favourite hour under the sun.

Botanical Garden

Honey, come, take a stroll with me
Beneath the winding beech branches
we can be alone.
Sunlight filters through the greenhouse roof
painting patterns on your face
your eyes squinting as you smile.
There are fish in the ponds
moving under the surface
like my adoration for you.

Let's rest under the birch trees,
and silently I hope for new beginnings;
Let me draw you as your face is in the sunlight
As your fingers strum the strings,
I'll make you a wreath of zingiber and bellflowers,
they'd look so pretty as your crown.
Let us fall asleep in a field of yellow orchids
even though I'd wish they were red or green,
and take a break from life that hates us so.

I only wish I had some starflowers

a little ounce of courage for the confession

a bit of the bravery you claim I possess

Just so I could take your hand

and meet your eye

and hand you a bundle of daffodils

Not that I'd ever dare

nor do I expect you to understand

or present me back with ragweeds or a rainflower.

My heart is yours, zingiber, covenlip toadflax,

but this garden's just a mauve carnation

Meet me in the botanical Garden

And let us get lost in artificial thicket

Darling, I give you my asters and

my red carnations

just for one of your rush daffodils;

You own my heart in gardenias,

but this path is full of marigolds.

My body is a Ghost

Some days my body is – wrong
Like I was switched up with someone else
like I am living my life from the back seat
with the shitty view.
Like my limbs are weighed down with lead
and my mouth is stuffed with cotton
and someone poured sand over my eyes
to prevent my control.

My body is a ghost,
my brain is on fire,
everything is topside down
and I -
Fuck, I just wanna breathe

I don't know what set it off
maybe an image, or a word,
or maybe I am simply to broken to fix,
but I am like a robot.

And everyone looks at me like

like I am supposed to – to know? To know what to do,

and I – I don't? So I must be

so I must be damaged, right?

My body is a ghost,

my brain is on fire,

everything is under water

and I -

I wish I didn't have to pretend.

Match/Gasoline

They say „It's the best thing to ever happen to you!"
But if that's true
I wanna know why it just hurts.
If there is nothing greater
Than falling in love,
Why feels every breath like I'm drowning,
Every word like I am starving?

If there's truly nothing greater
than falling in love
why does it hurt like a hellfire?
Sweetheart, I am gasoline,
and your smile is a match.

We can go weeks without talking
And I spend the in-betweens wondering
What I'll do if you grow tired of me
What I'd do if you don't come back?
And then I see the dots dancing,
see "Your Name is typing"

And my ears grow hot and I scramble to respond –
eating up every word like the air that I breathe;

If there is truly nothing greater
than being in love,
then why does it burn like a hellfire?
Sweetheart you're a match,
and I am gasoline.

Sister

We were supposed to be sisters –
a heart and a soul, born to be one.
You were my safe place, my haven,
then you betrayed my trust and trampled on my heart
until there were only shards and shambles left.
I was your guard, your place to stay,
a set of arms to hold you as you cried,
a voice to distract you from the aching.

What a sorry excuse for a friend you are
I gave you all, you took it and you spat it out
I drained my blood to keep you breathing
and your boot stood on my throat.

When you stood at my door at night
I took you in and I made you a bed
and I listened to you until your voice gave out,
and I guarded you from nightmares.
I chased your smile and your warmth,
Sucked up your "sister" like I was starving,
I'd never have given you up

and you knew and I bet it suited you
just fine to have a trashcan
who wouldn't talk back.

Why couldn't you just listen?
Why wouldn't you see that I was hurting?
That every dark sorrow I took off your chest
was attached to my heart and weighed it down -
I couldn't understand.

What a sorry excuse for a friend you are
Where I'd listen, you'd shut me out,
I kicked the water to keep you floating
and your weight dragged me down.

I bet that you preferred
Your loyal pet
Your "sister", no – your trashcan, a place to clean you shoes
before you went inside.

I bet you never thought
I'd catch on
My "sister", no – my vampire, my prison guard,
who only knows taking.

I am ridding myself of you,
Sister, sister, evil twin in my mirror,
Your words cut my wings and left me to die
But I grew a new set
And these ones have claws!

Clouds gather

I like to watch things from a window
Safely behind glass
Where I can see all but remain unseen,
Where I can't be hurt.

I wish I could leave behind my sorrow
Cover it with glass
But the truth is I cannot change what has been
Can't forget your word's burn.

You left me bruised and alone
A turtle without its shell
The snow collected in my hair –
I'm writing you off – I'm letting you die –
My life begins anew
And it will be brighter without you.

It took me a long time to get you go
And I didn't want to
I wanted the world to stay the way it was
Didn't realize I was breaking.

I took my time, but now that I know
I know what to do
You are a tumour, a scalpel will rid me of your mass
My real friends are my medicine.

You left me bruised and alone
A turtle without its shell
The storm was pulling my hair –
I'm writing you off – I'm letting you die
My life begins anew
And it will be brighter without you.

Without you – did you think I'd stay forever?!
When you tormented my soul?
Did you think I'd be forgiving?
You thought wrong!

'cause you left me bruised and alone
A turtle without its shell
The rain soaked through my hair –
I am writing you off – I'm letting you die –
My life begins anew
And it is brighter – without you.

Line 89 at 4 o'clock

There's a train
To take you far away,
You simply take the 89
A seat's reserved for you
And on and on you go.

The 89 goes anywhere,
A train to the Unknown,
You'll know it once you get there
A seat's reserved for you
And on and on you go.

There is no destination
For train line 89
Each passenger's got their own stop,
To jump off anytime.
A seat's reserved for you,
And on and on you go.

There's stops and go's
And heedless chaos
As you ride the 89
But don't you ever fret, my dear,
You will get there in time.
A seat has been reserved for you
Sit down and ride the line.

The train is long, the road is unfamiliar,
But we must each all ride it still
We'll all know when we get there
Look out of the window, see the world go by
We each must all ride this train
There is no reason why.

And it's possible line 89 goes nowhere
Maybe it's really standing still
But your seat's been reserved for you
And if you do not sit there
No-one ever will.

Flowers for you

If I dared to be a chrysanthemum
then I would give you daffodils
and lush red camellias.
However, I am red columbine
and you're a white gardenia.
Blue salvia,
red carnation
my dear –
I have tarragon and morning glory
and heaps of red carnations.
White clover, my love, white clover,
yellow tulips – and goodbye.